# High-Frequency Words Games LEVEL A
## Centers for Up to 6 Players

Editorial Development: Camille Liscinsky
Lisa Vitarisi Mathews
Copy Editing: Carrie Gwynne
Art Direction: Cheryl Puckett
Cover Design: Liliana Potigian
Illustration: Ann Iosa
Design/Production: Marcia Smith
Olivia C. Trinidad

EMC 3380

**Evan-Moor®**
EDUCATIONAL PUBLISHERS
*Helping Children Learn since 1979*

**Congratulations on your purchase of some of the finest teaching materials in the world.**

**Correlated** to State Standards

# Introduction

LEVEL A

## What Are High-Frequency Words?

High-frequency words, also called sight words, are words that students encounter frequently in reading and writing. Many of these words are referred to as "service words" because they are adjectives, adverbs, conjunctions, prepositions, and pronouns.

The words featured in *High-Frequency Words: Center Games for Up to 6 Players, Level A* come from the widely known and well-respected Dolch Word List.

### Dolch Pre-primer

| | | | |
|---|---|---|---|
| A | funny | make | three |
| a | go | me | to |
| and | help | my | two |
| away | here | not | up |
| big | I | one | we |
| blue | in | play | where |
| can | is | red | yellow |
| come | it | run | you |
| down | jump | said | |
| find | little | see | |
| for | look | the | |

### Dolch Primer

| | | | | |
|---|---|---|---|---|
| all | do | no | she | well |
| am | eat | now | so | went |
| are | four | on | soon | what |
| at | get | our | that | white |
| ate | good | out | there | who |
| be | have | please | they | will |
| black | he | pretty | this | with |
| brown | into | ran | too | yes |
| but | like | ride | under | |
| came | must | saw | want | |
| did | new | say | was | |

## Is Learning High-Frequency Words Important?

Many high-frequency words do not follow easy spelling patterns, making them difficult for students to master. Repeated practice is the key to knowing how to read and write these words. Students need to see the words, read the words, and write the words many, many times before they internalize them.

It is critical that students develop automaticity when reading high-frequency words. Automaticity, or fast, effortless, and accurate word recognition, grows out of repetition and practice. Games and activities using high-frequency words help students develop automaticity. Once students master high-frequency words, they are able to concentrate on other aspects of reading, such as comprehension.

 EMC 3380 • © Evan-Moor Corp.

# How to Use This Book

Have your students play the games to learn a variety of high-frequency words and to practice word recognition skills. The games are also fun "extra-time" or rainy-day recess activities. Model how to play each type of game, and place the games in an area of your classroom that is easily accessible to students.

## Games Include:

| Directions | Game boards | Game cards | Reproducible activity pages |
| --- | --- | --- | --- |

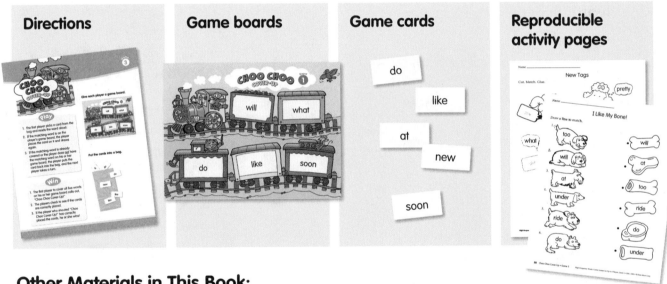

## Other Materials in This Book:

### Slider and Word Lists
The slider is a wonderful tool to help students master the high-frequency words practiced in the games.

### Word Wall Cutouts
Build a classroom word wall to provide a fun visual reference, as well as a starting point for a wide variety of word recognition activities.

# How to Prepare the Materials

## To Make a Center Game:

1. Laminate the directions page, the game boards, and the game cards.

2. Reproduce the activity pages.

3. Place the laminated game supplies and any additional items, such as bean markers or brown paper bags, in a folder that has a closure.

## You will need:

- laminator
- scissors
- brown paper bags
- game board markers (such as beans)
- folder with a closure

Directions page

Game boards

Game cards

Reproducible activity pages

## To Make the Word-List Slider:

1. Reproduce and cut out the slider on page 129, one for each student.

   *Note: You may wish to laminate the slider for durability.*

2. Reproduce the word lists on pages 130–134 for each student.

3. Have students cut the word lists apart and fasten them with a paper clip.

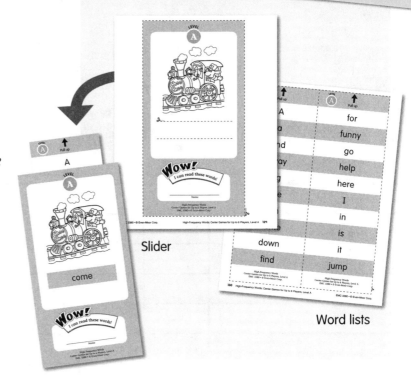

Slider

Word lists

## To Make the Word Wall:

1. Reproduce pages 135–143 and cut out the shapes.

2. Create a display like the one shown below.

# Games Checklist

**LEVEL A**

| Student | Games Played | Game 1 Word Match | Game 2 Concentration | Game 3 Choo Choo Cover-Up | Game 4 3-in-a-row Bingo | Game 5 Concentration | Game 6 Word Match | Game 7 Ping Pang Pow! |
|---|---|---|---|---|---|---|---|---|
|  |  |  |  |  |  |  |  |  |
|  |  |  |  |  |  |  |  |  |
|  |  |  |  |  |  |  |  |  |
|  |  |  |  |  |  |  |  |  |
|  |  |  |  |  |  |  |  |  |
|  |  |  |  |  |  |  |  |  |
|  |  |  |  |  |  |  |  |  |
|  |  |  |  |  |  |  |  |  |
|  |  |  |  |  |  |  |  |  |
|  |  |  |  |  |  |  |  |  |
|  |  |  |  |  |  |  |  |  |
|  |  |  |  |  |  |  |  |  |
|  |  |  |  |  |  |  |  |  |
|  |  |  |  |  |  |  |  |  |
|  |  |  |  |  |  |  |  |  |
|  |  |  |  |  |  |  |  |  |
|  |  |  |  |  |  |  |  |  |
|  |  |  |  |  |  |  |  |  |
|  |  |  |  |  |  |  |  |  |
|  |  |  |  |  |  |  |  |  |
|  |  |  |  |  |  |  |  |  |
|  |  |  |  |  |  |  |  |  |

# Word match

## play

1. Distribute the game boards and markers.
2. Put the caller's cards into the bag.
3. The caller picks a card from the bag, shows it to the players, reads the word aloud, and places it on the caller's board.
4. Players with the matching word on their boards place a marker on the word.
5. The caller picks a new card and play continues.

## Win

1. One or more players may win by covering all five words on their game boards. When all words are covered, the player or players call out, "I win!"
2. The player or players each read aloud the words on his or her game board as the caller checks the caller's board.
3. If the player's board and the caller's board match, the player wins!

## Each player needs:
- 1 game board
- Markers (such as beans)

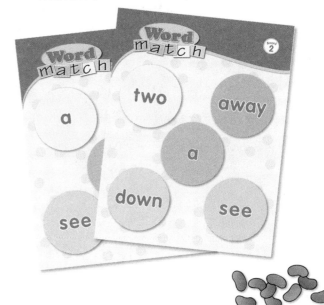

## The caller needs:
- Caller's board
- Caller's cards (includes upper- and lowercase *a*)
- Brown paper bag

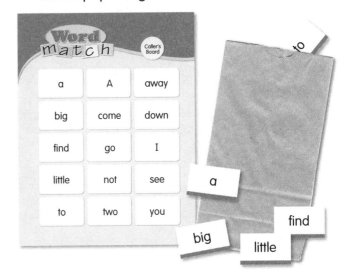

High-Frequency Words: Center Games for Up to 6 Players, Level A • EMC 3380 • © Evan-Moor Corp.

# Word match

a

away

find

see

not

## Game 1

High-Frequency Words
Center Games for Up to 6 Players, Level A
EMC 3380 • © Evan-Moor Corp.

# Word match

two

away

a

down

see

## Game 1

High-Frequency Words
Center Games for Up to 6 Players, Level A
EMC 3380 • © Evan-Moor Corp.

# Word match

come

see

away

big

a

## Game 1

High-Frequency Words
Center Games for Up to 6 Players, Level A
EMC 3380 • © Evan-Moor Corp.

# Word match

a

you

see

A

away

## Game 1

High-Frequency Words
Center Games for Up to 6 Players, Level A
EMC 3380 • © Evan-Moor Corp.

# Word match

away

I

little

see

a

## Game 1

High-Frequency Words
Center Games for Up to 6 Players, Level A
EMC 3380 • © Evan-Moor Corp.

# Word Match

away

see

go

a

to

## Game 1

High-Frequency Words
Center Games for Up to 6 Players, Level A
EMC 3380 • © Evan-Moor Corp.

## Caller's Cards

| a | A | away |
| --- | --- | --- |
| big | come | down |
| find | go | I |
| little | not | see |
| to | two | you |

### Game 1 • Caller's Cards

High-Frequency Words
Center Games for Up to 6 Players
Level A • EMC 3380 • © Evan-Moor Corp.

### Game 1 • Caller's Cards

High-Frequency Words
Center Games for Up to 6 Players
Level A • EMC 3380 • © Evan-Moor Corp.

### Game 1 • Caller's Cards

High-Frequency Words
Center Games for Up to 6 Players
Level A • EMC 3380 • © Evan-Moor Corp.

### Game 1 • Caller's Cards

High-Frequency Words
Center Games for Up to 6 Players
Level A • EMC 3380 • © Evan-Moor Corp.

### Game 1 • Caller's Cards

High-Frequency Words
Center Games for Up to 6 Players
Level A • EMC 3380 • © Evan-Moor Corp.

### Game 1 • Caller's Cards

High-Frequency Words
Center Games for Up to 6 Players
Level A • EMC 3380 • © Evan-Moor Corp.

### Game 1 • Caller's Cards

High-Frequency Words
Center Games for Up to 6 Players
Level A • EMC 3380 • © Evan-Moor Corp.

### Game 1 • Caller's Cards

High-Frequency Words
Center Games for Up to 6 Players
Level A • EMC 3380 • © Evan-Moor Corp.

### Game 1 • Caller's Cards

High-Frequency Words
Center Games for Up to 6 Players
Level A • EMC 3380 • © Evan-Moor Corp.

### Game 1 • Caller's Cards

High-Frequency Words
Center Games for Up to 6 Players
Level A • EMC 3380 • © Evan-Moor Corp.

### Game 1 • Caller's Cards

High-Frequency Words
Center Games for Up to 6 Players
Level A • EMC 3380 • © Evan-Moor Corp.

### Game 1 • Caller's Cards

High-Frequency Words
Center Games for Up to 6 Players
Level A • EMC 3380 • © Evan-Moor Corp.

### Game 1 • Caller's Cards

High-Frequency Words
Center Games for Up to 6 Players
Level A • EMC 3380 • © Evan-Moor Corp.

### Game 1 • Caller's Cards

High-Frequency Words
Center Games for Up to 6 Players
Level A • EMC 3380 • © Evan-Moor Corp.

### Game 1 • Caller's Cards

High-Frequency Words
Center Games for Up to 6 Players
Level A • EMC 3380 • © Evan-Moor Corp.

Word match

| a | A | away |
| big | come | down |
| find | go | I |
| little | not | see |
| to | two | you |

## Game 1

High-Frequency Words
Center Games for Up to 6 Players, Level A
EMC 3380 • © Evan-Moor Corp.

# I See You!

Cut. Match. Glue.

1.

4.

2.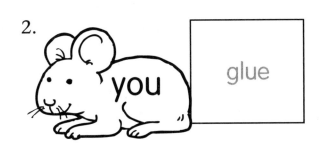

5.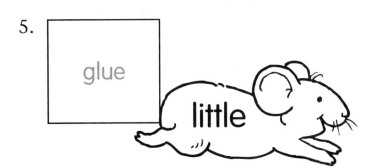

3.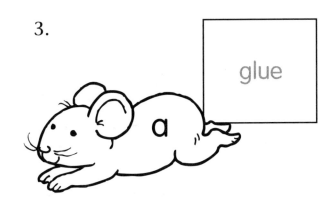

6.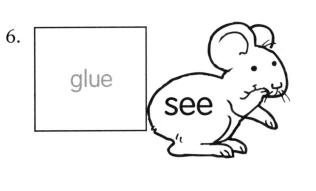

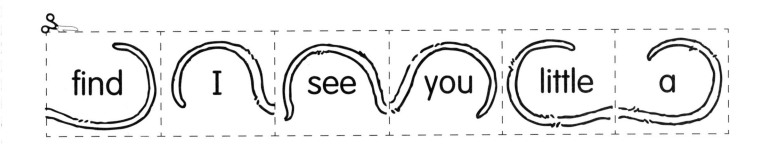

Name _____

# Food to Find

Draw a line to match.

1.

2.

3.

4.

5.

6.

  High-Frequency Words: Center Games for Up to 6 Players, Level A • EMC 3380 • © Evan-Moor Corp.

# Concentration

## Play

1. Place each set of cards facedown in six rows of four. Assign a group of three players to each set.

2. The first player in each group turns two cards over and reads the words aloud. If the words are the same, the player keeps the cards and plays again.

3. If the words are <u>not</u> the same, the player turns the cards over, and the next player takes a turn.

## Win

1. Play continues until all of the cards are matched.

2. Each player checks to make sure his or her cards are correctly matched.

3. The player with the most pairs wins!

**Set A players need:**

- 24 purple cards

**Set B players need:**

- 24 pink cards

High-Frequency Words: Center Games for Up to 6 Players, Level A • EMC 3380 • © Evan-Moor Corp.

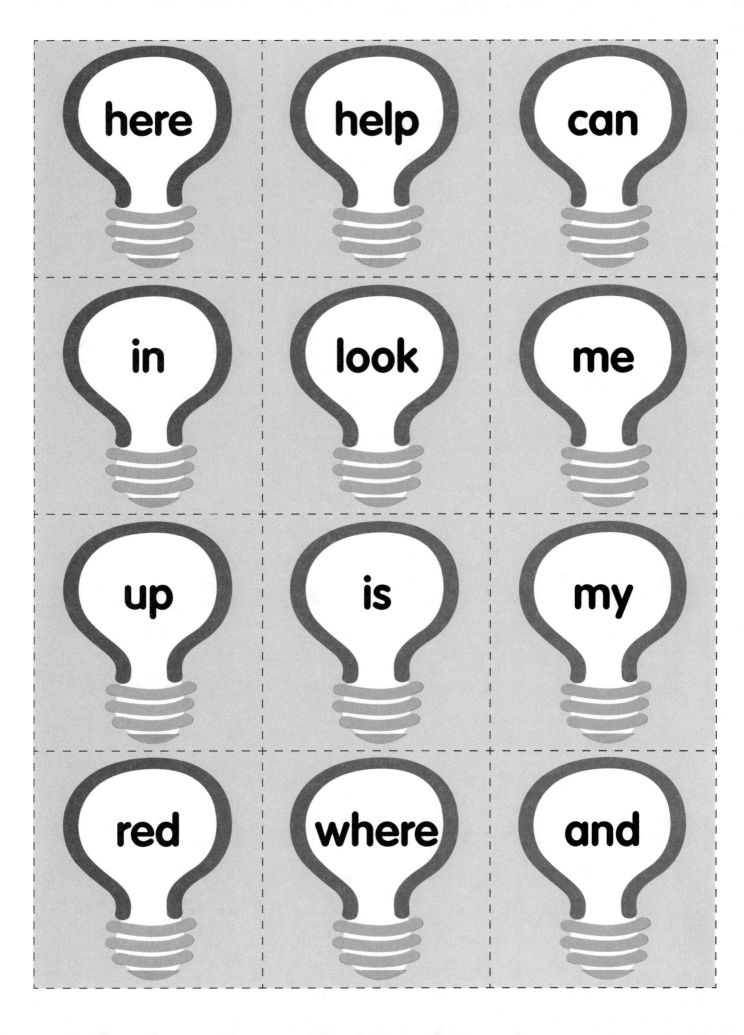

**Concentration**

## Game 2 • Set A

High-Frequency Words
Center Games for Up to 6 Players, Level A
EMC 3380 • © Evan-Moor Corp.

**Concentration**

## Game 2 • Set A

High-Frequency Words
Center Games for Up to 6 Players, Level A
EMC 3380 • © Evan-Moor Corp.

**Concentration**

## Game 2 • Set A

High-Frequency Words
Center Games for Up to 6 Players, Level A
EMC 3380 • © Evan-Moor Corp.

**Concentration**

## Game 2 • Set A

High-Frequency Words
Center Games for Up to 6 Players, Level A
EMC 3380 • © Evan-Moor Corp.

**Concentration**

## Game 2 • Set A

High-Frequency Words
Center Games for Up to 6 Players, Level A
EMC 3380 • © Evan-Moor Corp.

**Concentration**

## Game 2 • Set A

High-Frequency Words
Center Games for Up to 6 Players, Level A
EMC 3380 • © Evan-Moor Corp.

**Concentration**

## Game 2 • Set A

High-Frequency Words
Center Games for Up to 6 Players, Level A
EMC 3380 • © Evan-Moor Corp.

**Concentration**

## Game 2 • Set A

High-Frequency Words
Center Games for Up to 6 Players, Level A
EMC 3380 • © Evan-Moor Corp.

**Concentration**

## Game 2 • Set A

High-Frequency Words
Center Games for Up to 6 Players, Level A
EMC 3380 • © Evan-Moor Corp.

**Concentration**

## Game 2 • Set A

High-Frequency Words
Center Games for Up to 6 Players, Level A
EMC 3380 • © Evan-Moor Corp.

**Concentration**

## Game 2 • Set A

High-Frequency Words
Center Games for Up to 6 Players, Level A
EMC 3380 • © Evan-Moor Corp.

**Concentration**

## Game 2 • Set A

High-Frequency Words
Center Games for Up to 6 Players, Level A
EMC 3380 • © Evan-Moor Corp.

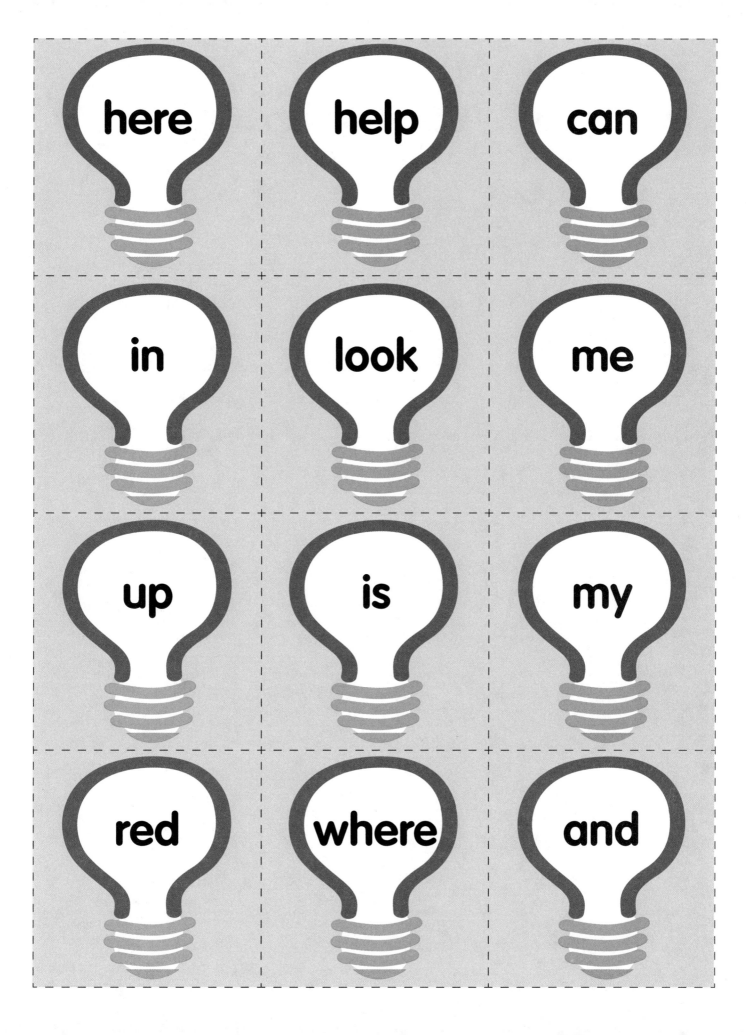

**Concentration**

## Game 2 • Set A

High-Frequency Words
Center Games for Up to 6 Players, Level A
EMC 3380 • © Evan-Moor Corp.

**Concentration**

## Game 2 • Set A

High-Frequency Words
Center Games for Up to 6 Players, Level A
EMC 3380 • © Evan-Moor Corp.

**Concentration**

## Game 2 • Set A

High-Frequency Words
Center Games for Up to 6 Players, Level A
EMC 3380 • © Evan-Moor Corp.

**Concentration**

## Game 2 • Set A

High-Frequency Words
Center Games for Up to 6 Players, Level A
EMC 3380 • © Evan-Moor Corp.

**Concentration**

## Game 2 • Set A

High-Frequency Words
Center Games for Up to 6 Players, Level A
EMC 3380 • © Evan-Moor Corp.

**Concentration**

## Game 2 • Set A

High-Frequency Words
Center Games for Up to 6 Players, Level A
EMC 3380 • © Evan-Moor Corp.

**Concentration**

## Game 2 • Set A

High-Frequency Words
Center Games for Up to 6 Players, Level A
EMC 3380 • © Evan-Moor Corp.

**Concentration**

## Game 2 • Set A

High-Frequency Words
Center Games for Up to 6 Players, Level A
EMC 3380 • © Evan-Moor Corp.

**Concentration**

## Game 2 • Set A

High-Frequency Words
Center Games for Up to 6 Players, Level A
EMC 3380 • © Evan-Moor Corp.

**Concentration**

## Game 2 • Set A

High-Frequency Words
Center Games for Up to 6 Players, Level A
EMC 3380 • © Evan-Moor Corp.

**Concentration**

## Game 2 • Set A

High-Frequency Words
Center Games for Up to 6 Players, Level A
EMC 3380 • © Evan-Moor Corp.

**Concentration**

## Game 2 • Set A

High-Frequency Words
Center Games for Up to 6 Players, Level A
EMC 3380 • © Evan-Moor Corp.

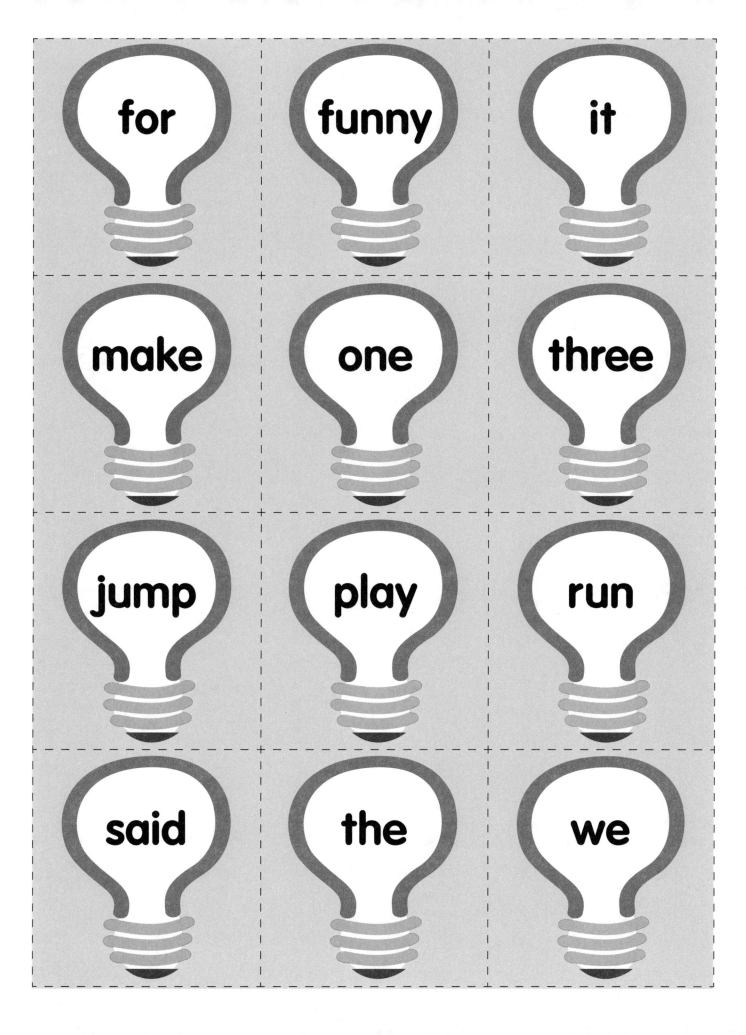

# Concentration

## Game 2 • Set B

High-Frequency Words
Center Games for Up to 6 Players, Level A
EMC 3380 • © Evan-Moor Corp.

# Concentration

## Game 2 • Set B

High-Frequency Words
Center Games for Up to 6 Players, Level A
EMC 3380 • © Evan-Moor Corp.

# Concentration

## Game 2 • Set B

High-Frequency Words
Center Games for Up to 6 Players, Level A
EMC 3380 • © Evan-Moor Corp.

# Concentration

## Game 2 • Set B

High-Frequency Words
Center Games for Up to 6 Players, Level A
EMC 3380 • © Evan-Moor Corp.

# Concentration

## Game 2 • Set B

High-Frequency Words
Center Games for Up to 6 Players, Level A
EMC 3380 • © Evan-Moor Corp.

# Concentration

## Game 2 • Set B

High-Frequency Words
Center Games for Up to 6 Players, Level A
EMC 3380 • © Evan-Moor Corp.

# Concentration

## Game 2 • Set B

High-Frequency Words
Center Games for Up to 6 Players, Level A
EMC 3380 • © Evan-Moor Corp.

# Concentration

## Game 2 • Set B

High-Frequency Words
Center Games for Up to 6 Players, Level A
EMC 3380 • © Evan-Moor Corp.

# Concentration

## Game 2 • Set B

High-Frequency Words
Center Games for Up to 6 Players, Level A
EMC 3380 • © Evan-Moor Corp.

# Concentration

## Game 2 • Set B

High-Frequency Words
Center Games for Up to 6 Players, Level A
EMC 3380 • © Evan-Moor Corp.

# Concentration

## Game 2 • Set B

High-Frequency Words
Center Games for Up to 6 Players, Level A
EMC 3380 • © Evan-Moor Corp.

# Concentration

## Game 2 • Set B

High-Frequency Words
Center Games for Up to 6 Players, Level A
EMC 3380 • © Evan-Moor Corp.

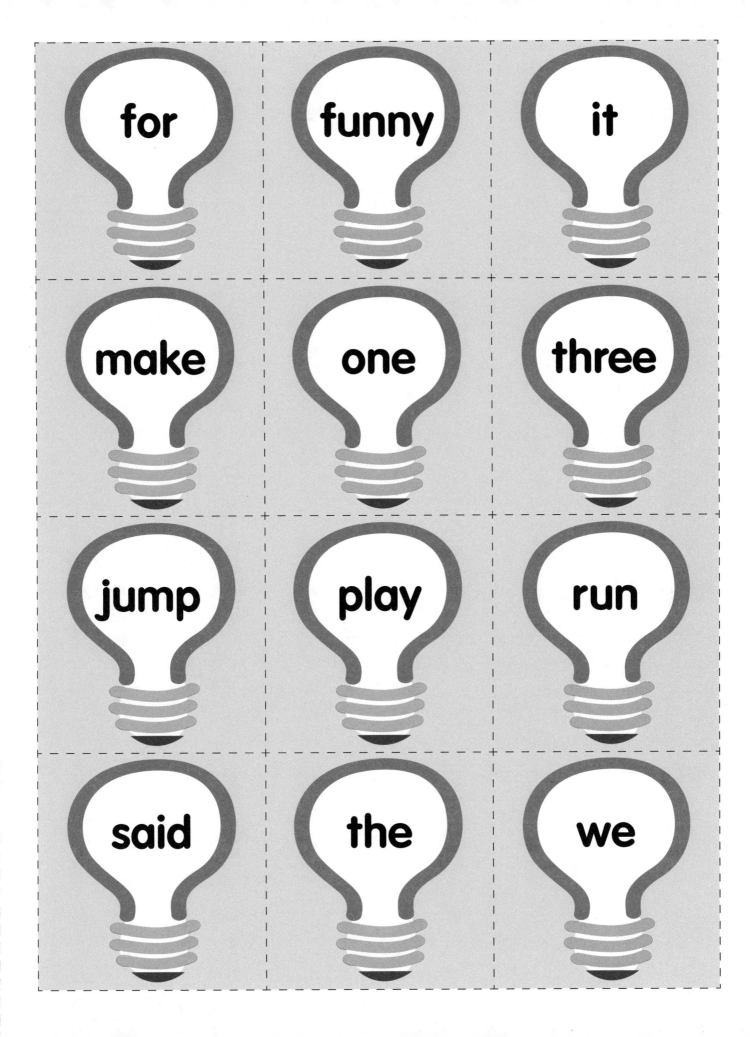

**Concentration**

Game 2 • Set B

High-Frequency Words
Center Games for Up to 6 Players, Level A
EMC 3380 • © Evan-Moor Corp.

**Concentration**

Game 2 • Set B

High-Frequency Words
Center Games for Up to 6 Players, Level A
EMC 3380 • © Evan-Moor Corp.

**Concentration**

Game 2 • Set B

High-Frequency Words
Center Games for Up to 6 Players, Level A
EMC 3380 • © Evan-Moor Corp.

**Concentration**

Game 2 • Set B

High-Frequency Words
Center Games for Up to 6 Players, Level A
EMC 3380 • © Evan-Moor Corp.

**Concentration**

Game 2 • Set B

High-Frequency Words
Center Games for Up to 6 Players, Level A
EMC 3380 • © Evan-Moor Corp.

**Concentration**

Game 2 • Set B

High-Frequency Words
Center Games for Up to 6 Players, Level A
EMC 3380 • © Evan-Moor Corp.

**Concentration**

Game 2 • Set B

High-Frequency Words
Center Games for Up to 6 Players, Level A
EMC 3380 • © Evan-Moor Corp.

**Concentration**

Game 2 • Set B

High-Frequency Words
Center Games for Up to 6 Players, Level A
EMC 3380 • © Evan-Moor Corp.

**Concentration**

Game 2 • Set B

High-Frequency Words
Center Games for Up to 6 Players, Level A
EMC 3380 • © Evan-Moor Corp.

**Concentration**

Game 2 • Set B

High-Frequency Words
Center Games for Up to 6 Players, Level A
EMC 3380 • © Evan-Moor Corp.

**Concentration**

Game 2 • Set B

High-Frequency Words
Center Games for Up to 6 Players, Level A
EMC 3380 • © Evan-Moor Corp.

**Concentration**

Game 2 • Set B

High-Frequency Words
Center Games for Up to 6 Players, Level A
EMC 3380 • © Evan-Moor Corp.

Name _____

# Duck in a Tub

Cut. Match. Glue.

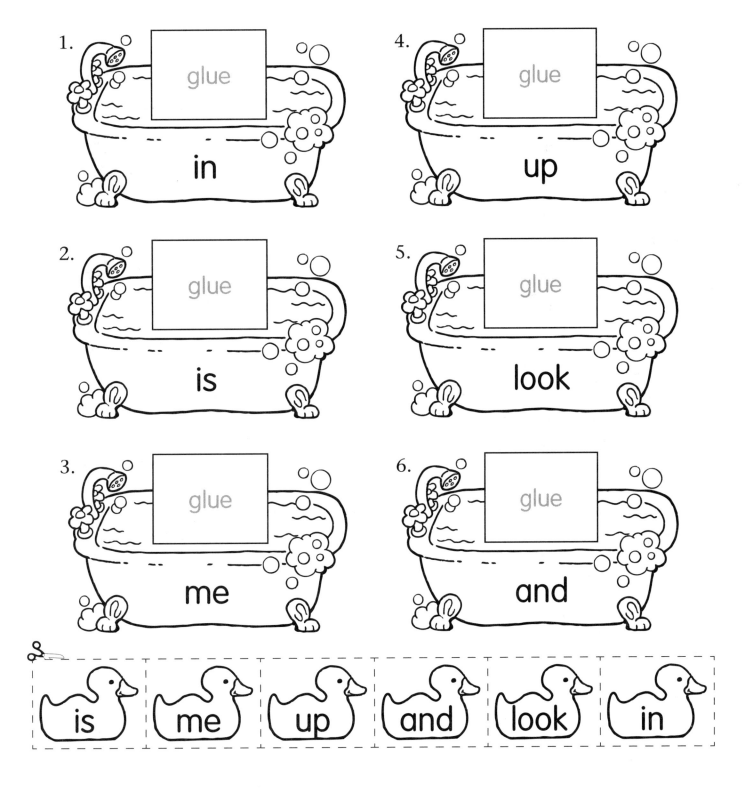

1. glue

in

2. glue

is

3. glue

me

4. glue

up

5. glue

look

6. glue

and

is   me   up   and   look   in

Name _____

# Where Is My Bug?

Draw a line to match.

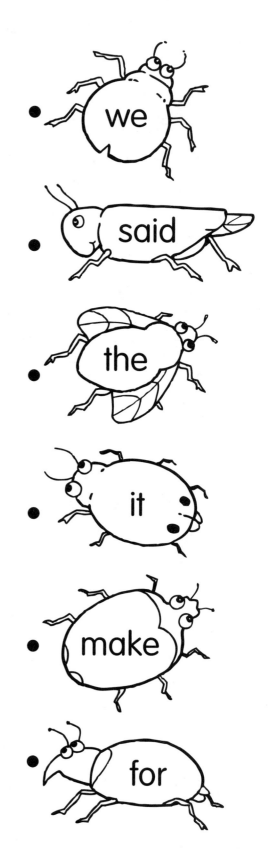

1. said
2. the
3. we
4. for
5. it
6. make

we
said
the
it
make
for

# Choo Choo Cover-Up

## Play

1. The first player picks a card from the bag and reads the word aloud.

2. If the matching word is on the player's game board, the player places the card on it and draws again.

3. If the matching word is already covered or the player does <u>not</u> have the matching word on his or her game board, the player puts the card back into the bag, and the next player takes a turn.

## Win

1. The first player to cover all five words on his or her game board calls out, "Choo Choo Cover-Up!"

2. The players check to see if the cards are correctly placed.

3. If the player who shouted "Choo Choo Cover-Up!" has correctly placed the cards, he or she wins!

**Give each player a game board.**

**Put the cards into a bag.**

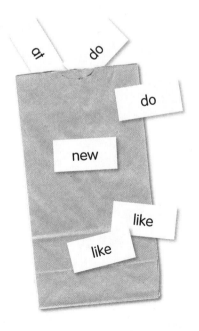

# Game 3

High-Frequency Words
Center Games for Up to 6 Players, Level A
EMC 3380 • © Evan-Moor Corp.

# Game 3

High-Frequency Words
Center Games for Up to 6 Players, Level A
EMC 3380 • © Evan-Moor Corp.

# Game 3

High-Frequency Words
Center Games for Up to 6 Players, Level A
EMC 3380 • © Evan-Moor Corp.

# Game 3

High-Frequency Words
Center Games for Up to 6 Players, Level A
EMC 3380 • © Evan-Moor Corp.

# Game 3

High-Frequency Words
Center Games for Up to 6 Players, Level A
EMC 3380 • © Evan-Moor Corp.

# Game 3

High-Frequency Words
Center Games for Up to 6 Players, Level A
EMC 3380 • © Evan-Moor Corp.

| do | do | do |
|----|----|----|
| do | do | do |
| like | like | like |
| like | like | like |
| at | at | at |
| new | new | new |

**Game 3**
High-Frequency Words
Center Games for Up to 6 Players
Level A • EMC 3380 • © Evan-Moor Corp.

**Game 3**
High-Frequency Words
Center Games for Up to 6 Players
Level A • EMC 3380 • © Evan-Moor Corp.

**Game 3**
High-Frequency Words
Center Games for Up to 6 Players
Level A • EMC 3380 • © Evan-Moor Corp.

**Game 3**
High-Frequency Words
Center Games for Up to 6 Players
Level A • EMC 3380 • © Evan-Moor Corp.

**Game 3**
High-Frequency Words
Center Games for Up to 6 Players
Level A • EMC 3380 • © Evan-Moor Corp.

**Game 3**
High-Frequency Words
Center Games for Up to 6 Players
Level A • EMC 3380 • © Evan-Moor Corp.

**Game 3**
High-Frequency Words
Center Games for Up to 6 Players
Level A • EMC 3380 • © Evan-Moor Corp.

**Game 3**
High-Frequency Words
Center Games for Up to 6 Players
Level A • EMC 3380 • © Evan-Moor Corp.

**Game 3**
High-Frequency Words
Center Games for Up to 6 Players
Level A • EMC 3380 • © Evan-Moor Corp.

**Game 3**
High-Frequency Words
Center Games for Up to 6 Players
Level A • EMC 3380 • © Evan-Moor Corp.

**Game 3**
High-Frequency Words
Center Games for Up to 6 Players
Level A • EMC 3380 • © Evan-Moor Corp.

**Game 3**
High-Frequency Words
Center Games for Up to 6 Players
Level A • EMC 3380 • © Evan-Moor Corp.

**Game 3**
High-Frequency Words
Center Games for Up to 6 Players
Level A • EMC 3380 • © Evan-Moor Corp.

**Game 3**
High-Frequency Words
Center Games for Up to 6 Players
Level A • EMC 3380 • © Evan-Moor Corp.

**Game 3**
High-Frequency Words
Center Games for Up to 6 Players
Level A • EMC 3380 • © Evan-Moor Corp.

**Game 3**
High-Frequency Words
Center Games for Up to 6 Players
Level A • EMC 3380 • © Evan-Moor Corp.

**Game 3**
High-Frequency Words
Center Games for Up to 6 Players
Level A • EMC 3380 • © Evan-Moor Corp.

**Game 3**
High-Frequency Words
Center Games for Up to 6 Players
Level A • EMC 3380 • © Evan-Moor Corp.

| too | too | too |
|-----|-----|-----|
| what | what | what |
| will | will | will |
| under | under | under |
| pretty | pretty | ride |
| ride | soon | soon |

**Game 3**
High-Frequency Words
Center Games for Up to 6 Players
Level A • EMC 3380 • © Evan-Moor Corp.

**Game 3**
High-Frequency Words
Center Games for Up to 6 Players
Level A • EMC 3380 • © Evan-Moor Corp.

**Game 3**
High-Frequency Words
Center Games for Up to 6 Players
Level A • EMC 3380 • © Evan-Moor Corp.

**Game 3**
High-Frequency Words
Center Games for Up to 6 Players
Level A • EMC 3380 • © Evan-Moor Corp.

**Game 3**
High-Frequency Words
Center Games for Up to 6 Players
Level A • EMC 3380 • © Evan-Moor Corp.

**Game 3**
High-Frequency Words
Center Games for Up to 6 Players
Level A • EMC 3380 • © Evan-Moor Corp.

**Game 3**
High-Frequency Words
Center Games for Up to 6 Players
Level A • EMC 3380 • © Evan-Moor Corp.

**Game 3**
High-Frequency Words
Center Games for Up to 6 Players
Level A • EMC 3380 • © Evan-Moor Corp.

**Game 3**
High-Frequency Words
Center Games for Up to 6 Players
Level A • EMC 3380 • © Evan-Moor Corp.

**Game 3**
High-Frequency Words
Center Games for Up to 6 Players
Level A • EMC 3380 • © Evan-Moor Corp.

**Game 3**
High-Frequency Words
Center Games for Up to 6 Players
Level A • EMC 3380 • © Evan-Moor Corp.

**Game 3**
High-Frequency Words
Center Games for Up to 6 Players
Level A • EMC 3380 • © Evan-Moor Corp.

**Game 3**
High-Frequency Words
Center Games for Up to 6 Players
Level A • EMC 3380 • © Evan-Moor Corp.

**Game 3**
High-Frequency Words
Center Games for Up to 6 Players
Level A • EMC 3380 • © Evan-Moor Corp.

**Game 3**
High-Frequency Words
Center Games for Up to 6 Players
Level A • EMC 3380 • © Evan-Moor Corp.

**Game 3**
High-Frequency Words
Center Games for Up to 6 Players
Level A • EMC 3380 • © Evan-Moor Corp.

**Game 3**
High-Frequency Words
Center Games for Up to 6 Players
Level A • EMC 3380 • © Evan-Moor Corp.

**Game 3**
High-Frequency Words
Center Games for Up to 6 Players
Level A • EMC 3380 • © Evan-Moor Corp.

# New Tags

Cut. Match. Glue.

Name _____

# I Like My Bone!

Draw a line to match.

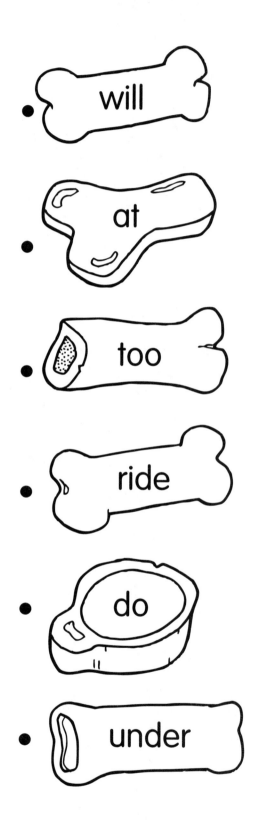

   High-Frequency Words: Center Games for Up to 6 Players, Level A • EMC 3380 • © Evan-Moor Corp.

# 3 in-a-row BINGO

## Play

1. Players cover the FREE space on their game boards with a marker.

2. The caller picks a card from the bag, shows it to the players, reads the word aloud, and places it on the caller's board.

3. Players look for the word on their game boards. If they find the word, they cover it with a marker.

4. The caller picks another card from the bag and play continues.

## Win

1. One or more players may win by covering each word in a single row. The row can go down, across, or diagonally.

2. The first player or players to cover all the words in a row calls out, "Bingo!"

3. The player or players each read aloud the words in the row as the caller checks the caller's board.

4. If the player's board and the caller's board match, the player wins!

### Each player needs:
- 1 game board
- Markers (such as beans)

### The caller needs:
- Caller's board
- Caller's cards

#### Caller's Board
#### 3 in-a-row BINGO

| all | but | came |
|------|------|------|
| did | get | good |
| have | look | must |
| now | say | there |
| this | up | want |
| was | who | yes |

### Put the cards into a bag.

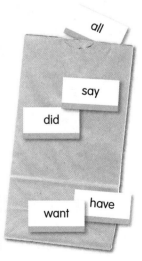

# 3 in-a-row

# BINGO

| | | |
|---|---|---|
| have | but | this |
| all | FREE | say |
| good | was | yes |

## Game 4

High-Frequency Words
Center Games for Up to 6 Players, Level A
EMC 3380 • © Evan-Moor Corp.

| | | |
|---|---|---|
| who | now | there |
| want | FREE | good |
| say | yes | get |

## Game 4

High-Frequency Words
Center Games for Up to 6 Players, Level A
EMC 3380 • © Evan-Moor Corp.

# BINGO

| | | |
|---|---|---|
| this | up | have |
| look | FREE | want |
| was | good | all |

# Game 4

High-Frequency Words
Center Games for Up to 6 Players, Level A
EMC 3380 • © Evan-Moor Corp.

# 3 in-a-row BINGO

| | | |
|---|---|---|
| did | was | but |
| have | FREE | came |
| up | must | this |

## Game 4

High-Frequency Words
Center Games for Up to 6 Players, Level A
EMC 3380 • © Evan-Moor Corp.

| | | |
|---|---|---|
| get | have | must |
| but | FREE | who |
| did | all | there |

## Game 4

High-Frequency Words
Center Games for Up to 6 Players, Level A
EMC 3380 • © Evan-Moor Corp.

# 3 in-a-row
# BINGO

Board 6

| | | |
|---|---|---|
| say | now | want |
| came | FREE | there |
| who | get | look |

## Game 4

High-Frequency Words
Center Games for Up to 6 Players, Level A
EMC 3380 • © Evan-Moor Corp.

Caller's Cards

| all | but | came |
| did | get | good |
| have | must | now |
| say | there | this |
| want | was | who |
| yes | up | look |

## Game 4 • Caller's Cards

High-Frequency Words
Center Games for Up to 6 Players
Level A • EMC 3380 • © Evan-Moor Corp.

## Game 4 • Caller's Cards

High-Frequency Words
Center Games for Up to 6 Players
Level A • EMC 3380 • © Evan-Moor Corp.

## Game 4 • Caller's Cards

High-Frequency Words
Center Games for Up to 6 Players
Level A • EMC 3380 • © Evan-Moor Corp.

## Game 4 • Caller's Cards

High-Frequency Words
Center Games for Up to 6 Players
Level A • EMC 3380 • © Evan-Moor Corp.

## Game 4 • Caller's Cards

High-Frequency Words
Center Games for Up to 6 Players
Level A • EMC 3380 • © Evan-Moor Corp.

## Game 4 • Caller's Cards

High-Frequency Words
Center Games for Up to 6 Players
Level A • EMC 3380 • © Evan-Moor Corp.

## Game 4 • Caller's Cards

High-Frequency Words
Center Games for Up to 6 Players
Level A • EMC 3380 • © Evan-Moor Corp.

## Game 4 • Caller's Cards

High-Frequency Words
Center Games for Up to 6 Players
Level A • EMC 3380 • © Evan-Moor Corp.

## Game 4 • Caller's Cards

High-Frequency Words
Center Games for Up to 6 Players
Level A • EMC 3380 • © Evan-Moor Corp.

## Game 4 • Caller's Cards

High-Frequency Words
Center Games for Up to 6 Players
Level A • EMC 3380 • © Evan-Moor Corp.

## Game 4 • Caller's Cards

High-Frequency Words
Center Games for Up to 6 Players
Level A • EMC 3380 • © Evan-Moor Corp.

## Game 4 • Caller's Cards

High-Frequency Words
Center Games for Up to 6 Players
Level A • EMC 3380 • © Evan-Moor Corp.

## Game 4 • Caller's Cards

High-Frequency Words
Center Games for Up to 6 Players
Level A • EMC 3380 • © Evan-Moor Corp.

## Game 4 • Caller's Cards

High-Frequency Words
Center Games for Up to 6 Players
Level A • EMC 3380 • © Evan-Moor Corp.

## Game 4 • Caller's Cards

High-Frequency Words
Center Games for Up to 6 Players
Level A • EMC 3380 • © Evan-Moor Corp.

## Game 4 • Caller's Cards

High-Frequency Words
Center Games for Up to 6 Players
Level A • EMC 3380 • © Evan-Moor Corp.

## Game 4 • Caller's Cards

High-Frequency Words
Center Games for Up to 6 Players
Level A • EMC 3380 • © Evan-Moor Corp.

## Game 4 • Caller's Cards

High-Frequency Words
Center Games for Up to 6 Players
Level A • EMC 3380 • © Evan-Moor Corp.

Caller's Board

**3 in-a-row**

# BINGO

| all | but | came |
|-----|-----|------|
| did | get | good |
| have | look | must |
| now | say | there |
| this | up | want |
| was | who | yes |

## Game 4

High-Frequency Words
Center Games for Up to 6 Players, Level A
EMC 3380 • © Evan-Moor Corp.

Name _____

# Get My Wing!

Cut. Match. Glue.

Name _____

# This Is Good!

Draw a line to match.

1.

2.

3.

4.

5.

6.

 High-Frequency Words: Center Games for Up to 6 Players, Level A • EMC 3380 • © Evan-Moor Corp.

# Concentration

## Play

1. Place each set of cards facedown in six rows of four. Assign a group of three players to each set.

2. The first player in each group turns two cards over and reads the words aloud. If the words match, the player keeps the cards and plays again.

3. If the words do <u>not</u> match, the player turns the cards over, and the next player takes a turn.

**Set A players need:**

• 24 green cards

## Win

1. Play continues until all of the cards are matched.

2. Each player checks to make sure his or her cards are correctly matched.

3. The player with the most pairs wins!

**Set B players need:**

• 24 pink cards

High-Frequency Words: Center Games for Up to 6 Players, Level A • EMC 3380 • © Evan-Moor Corp.

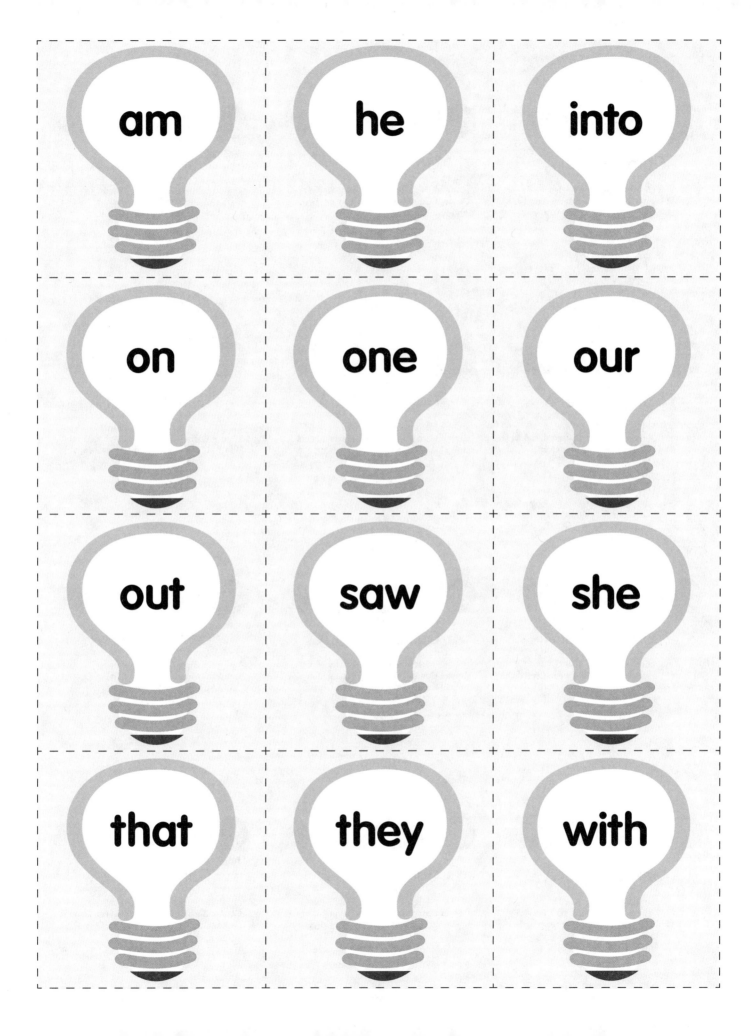

## Game 5 • Set A

High-Frequency Words
Center Games for Up to 6 Players, Level A
EMC 3380 • © Evan-Moor Corp.

## Game 5 • Set A

High-Frequency Words
Center Games for Up to 6 Players, Level A
EMC 3380 • © Evan-Moor Corp.

## Game 5 • Set A

High-Frequency Words
Center Games for Up to 6 Players, Level A
EMC 3380 • © Evan-Moor Corp.

## Game 5 • Set A

High-Frequency Words
Center Games for Up to 6 Players, Level A
EMC 3380 • © Evan-Moor Corp.

## Game 5 • Set A

High-Frequency Words
Center Games for Up to 6 Players, Level A
EMC 3380 • © Evan-Moor Corp.

## Game 5 • Set A

High-Frequency Words
Center Games for Up to 6 Players, Level A
EMC 3380 • © Evan-Moor Corp.

## Game 5 • Set A

High-Frequency Words
Center Games for Up to 6 Players, Level A
EMC 3380 • © Evan-Moor Corp.

## Game 5 • Set A

High-Frequency Words
Center Games for Up to 6 Players, Level A
EMC 3380 • © Evan-Moor Corp.

## Game 5 • Set A

High-Frequency Words
Center Games for Up to 6 Players, Level A
EMC 3380 • © Evan-Moor Corp.

## Game 5 • Set A

High-Frequency Words
Center Games for Up to 6 Players, Level A
EMC 3380 • © Evan-Moor Corp.

## Game 5 • Set A

High-Frequency Words
Center Games for Up to 6 Players, Level A
EMC 3380 • © Evan-Moor Corp.

## Game 5 • Set A

High-Frequency Words
Center Games for Up to 6 Players, Level A
EMC 3380 • © Evan-Moor Corp.

## Game 5 • Set A

High-Frequency Words
Center Games for Up to 6 Players, Level A
EMC 3380 • © Evan-Moor Corp.

## Game 5 • Set A

High-Frequency Words
Center Games for Up to 6 Players, Level A
EMC 3380 • © Evan-Moor Corp.

## Game 5 • Set A

High-Frequency Words
Center Games for Up to 6 Players, Level A
EMC 3380 • © Evan-Moor Corp.

## Game 5 • Set A

High-Frequency Words
Center Games for Up to 6 Players, Level A
EMC 3380 • © Evan-Moor Corp.

## Game 5 • Set A

High-Frequency Words
Center Games for Up to 6 Players, Level A
EMC 3380 • © Evan-Moor Corp.

## Game 5 • Set A

High-Frequency Words
Center Games for Up to 6 Players, Level A
EMC 3380 • © Evan-Moor Corp.

## Game 5 • Set A

High-Frequency Words
Center Games for Up to 6 Players, Level A
EMC 3380 • © Evan-Moor Corp.

## Game 5 • Set A

High-Frequency Words
Center Games for Up to 6 Players, Level A
EMC 3380 • © Evan-Moor Corp.

## Game 5 • Set A

High-Frequency Words
Center Games for Up to 6 Players, Level A
EMC 3380 • © Evan-Moor Corp.

## Game 5 • Set A

High-Frequency Words
Center Games for Up to 6 Players, Level A
EMC 3380 • © Evan-Moor Corp.

## Game 5 • Set A

High-Frequency Words
Center Games for Up to 6 Players, Level A
EMC 3380 • © Evan-Moor Corp.

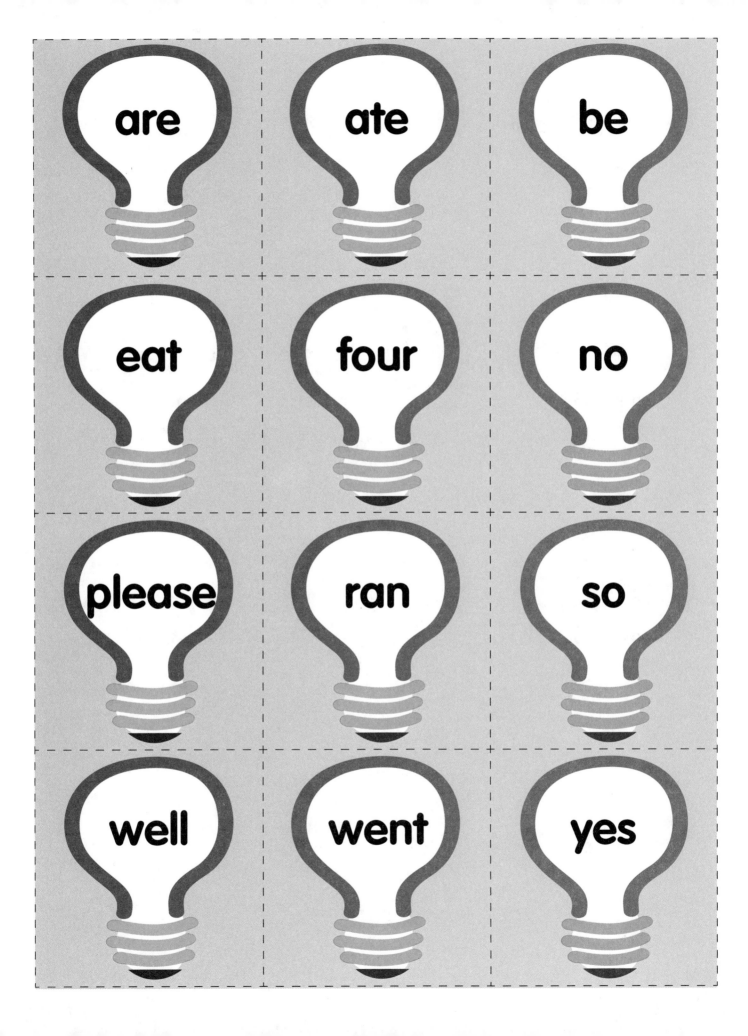

## Concentration

### Game 5 • Set B

High-Frequency Words
Center Games for Up to 6 Players, Level A
EMC 3380 • © Evan-Moor Corp.

## Concentration

### Game 5 • Set B

High-Frequency Words
Center Games for Up to 6 Players, Level A
EMC 3380 • © Evan-Moor Corp.

## Concentration

### Game 5 • Set B

High-Frequency Words
Center Games for Up to 6 Players, Level A
EMC 3380 • © Evan-Moor Corp.

## Concentration

### Game 5 • Set B

High-Frequency Words
Center Games for Up to 6 Players, Level A
EMC 3380 • © Evan-Moor Corp.

## Concentration

### Game 5 • Set B

High-Frequency Words
Center Games for Up to 6 Players, Level A
EMC 3380 • © Evan-Moor Corp.

## Concentration

### Game 5 • Set B

High-Frequency Words
Center Games for Up to 6 Players, Level A
EMC 3380 • © Evan-Moor Corp.

## Concentration

### Game 5 • Set B

High-Frequency Words
Center Games for Up to 6 Players, Level A
EMC 3380 • © Evan-Moor Corp.

## Concentration

### Game 5 • Set B

High-Frequency Words
Center Games for Up to 6 Players, Level A
EMC 3380 • © Evan-Moor Corp.

## Concentration

### Game 5 • Set B

High-Frequency Words
Center Games for Up to 6 Players, Level A
EMC 3380 • © Evan-Moor Corp.

## Concentration

### Game 5 • Set B

High-Frequency Words
Center Games for Up to 6 Players, Level A
EMC 3380 • © Evan-Moor Corp.

## Concentration

### Game 5 • Set B

High-Frequency Words
Center Games for Up to 6 Players, Level A
EMC 3380 • © Evan-Moor Corp.

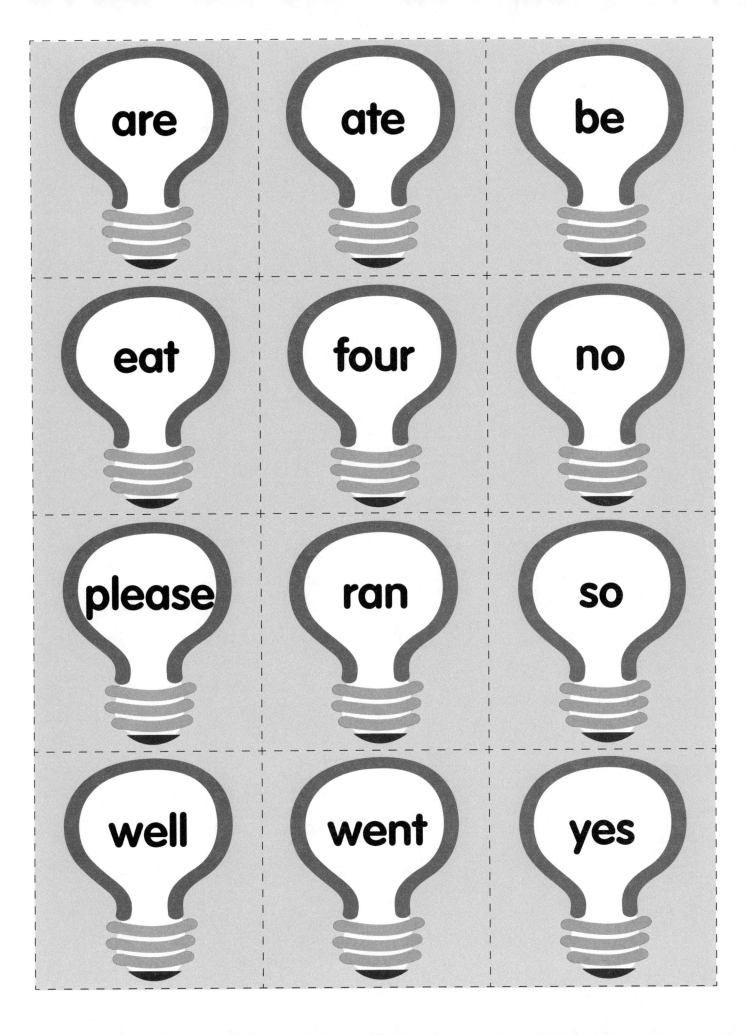

## Concentration

### Game 5 • Set B

High-Frequency Words
Center Games for Up to 6 Players, Level A
EMC 3380 • © Evan-Moor Corp.

## Concentration

### Game 5 • Set B

High-Frequency Words
Center Games for Up to 6 Players, Level A
EMC 3380 • © Evan-Moor Corp.

## Concentration

### Game 5 • Set B

High-Frequency Words
Center Games for Up to 6 Players, Level A
EMC 3380 • © Evan-Moor Corp.

## Concentration

### Game 5 • Set B

High-Frequency Words
Center Games for Up to 6 Players, Level A
EMC 3380 • © Evan-Moor Corp.

## Concentration

### Game 5 • Set B

High-Frequency Words
Center Games for Up to 6 Players, Level A
EMC 3380 • © Evan-Moor Corp.

## Concentration

### Game 5 • Set B

High-Frequency Words
Center Games for Up to 6 Players, Level A
EMC 3380 • © Evan-Moor Corp.

## Concentration

### Game 5 • Set B

High-Frequency Words
Center Games for Up to 6 Players, Level A
EMC 3380 • © Evan-Moor Corp.

## Concentration

### Game 5 • Set B

High-Frequency Words
Center Games for Up to 6 Players, Level A
EMC 3380 • © Evan-Moor Corp.

## Concentration

### Game 5 • Set B

High-Frequency Words
Center Games for Up to 6 Players, Level A
EMC 3380 • © Evan-Moor Corp.

## Concentration

### Game 5 • Set B

High-Frequency Words
Center Games for Up to 6 Players, Level A
EMC 3380 • © Evan-Moor Corp.

## Concentration

### Game 5 • Set B

High-Frequency Words
Center Games for Up to 6 Players, Level A
EMC 3380 • © Evan-Moor Corp.

## Concentration

### Game 5 • Set B

High-Frequency Words
Center Games for Up to 6 Players, Level A
EMC 3380 • © Evan-Moor Corp.

# They Want a Fin!

Cut. Match. Glue.

he    our    am    she    that    they

# They Eat Fish

Draw a line to match.

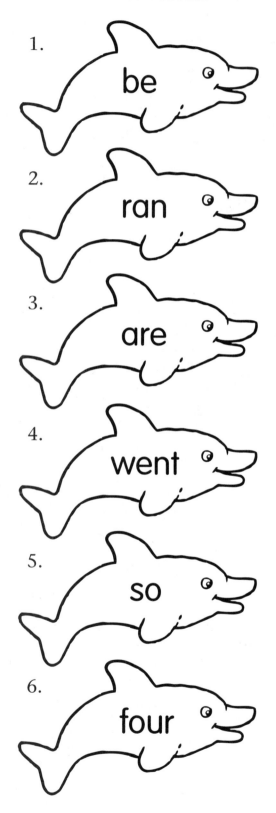

1. be

2. ran

3. are

4. went

5. so

6. four

- are

- be

- so

- ran

- four

- went

# Word match

## play

1. Distribute the game boards and markers.
2. Put the caller's cards into the bag.
3. The caller picks a card from the bag, shows it to the players, reads the word aloud, and places it on the caller's board.
4. Players with the matching word on their boards place a marker on the word.
5. The caller picks a new card and play continues.

## Win

1. One or more players may win by covering all five words on their game boards. When all words are covered, the player or players call out, "I win!"
2. The player or players each read aloud the words on his or her game board as the caller checks the caller's board.
3. If the player's board and the caller's board match, the player wins!

## Each player needs:

- 1 game board
- Markers (such as beans)

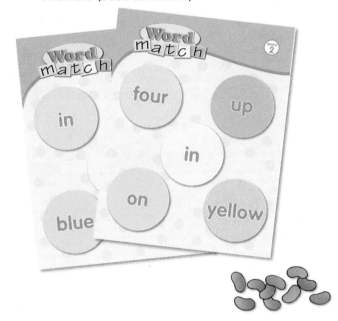

## The caller needs:

- Caller's board
- Caller's cards
- Brown paper bag

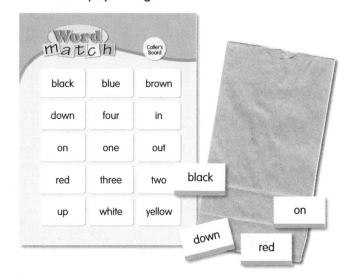

High-Frequency Words: Center Games for Up to 6 Players, Level A • EMC 3380 • © Evan-Moor Corp.

# Word match

in

one

up

blue

on

## Game 6

High-Frequency Words
Center Games for Up to 6 Players, Level A
EMC 3380 • © Evan-Moor Corp.

# Word match

four

up

in

on

yellow

## Game 6

High-Frequency Words
Center Games for Up to 6 Players, Level A
EMC 3380 • © Evan-Moor Corp.

# Word match

black

in

out

on

up

## Game 6

High-Frequency Words
Center Games for Up to 6 Players, Level A
EMC 3380 • © Evan-Moor Corp.

# Word match

red

up

two

in

on

## Game 6

High-Frequency Words
Center Games for Up to 6 Players, Level A
EMC 3380 • © Evan-Moor Corp.

# Word match

on

in

up

three

white

## Game 6

High-Frequency Words
Center Games for Up to 6 Players, Level A
EMC 3380 • © Evan-Moor Corp.

# Word match

up

down

on

in

brown

# Game 6

High-Frequency Words
Center Games for Up to 6 Players, Level A
EMC 3380 • © Evan-Moor Corp.

| black | blue | brown |
|-------|------|-------|
| down | four | in |
| on | one | out |
| red | three | two |
| up | white | yellow |

### Game 6 • Caller's Cards

High-Frequency Words
Center Games for Up to 6 Players,
Level A • EMC 3380 • © Evan-Moor Corp.

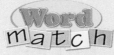

### Game 6 • Caller's Cards

High-Frequency Words
Center Games for Up to 6 Players,
Level A • EMC 3380 • © Evan-Moor Corp.

### Game 6 • Caller's Cards

High-Frequency Words
Center Games for Up to 6 Players,
Level A • EMC 3380 • © Evan-Moor Corp.

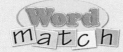

### Game 6 • Caller's Cards

High-Frequency Words
Center Games for Up to 6 Players,
Level A • EMC 3380 • © Evan-Moor Corp.

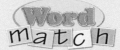

### Game 6 • Caller's Cards

High-Frequency Words
Center Games for Up to 6 Players,
Level A • EMC 3380 • © Evan-Moor Corp.

### Game 6 • Caller's Cards

High-Frequency Words
Center Games for Up to 6 Players,
Level A • EMC 3380 • © Evan-Moor Corp.

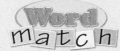

### Game 6 • Caller's Cards

High-Frequency Words
Center Games for Up to 6 Players,
Level A • EMC 3380 • © Evan-Moor Corp.

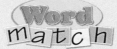

### Game 6 • Caller's Cards

High-Frequency Words
Center Games for Up to 6 Players,
Level A • EMC 3380 • © Evan-Moor Corp.

### Game 6 • Caller's Cards

High-Frequency Words
Center Games for Up to 6 Players,
Level A • EMC 3380 • © Evan-Moor Corp.

### Game 6 • Caller's Cards

High-Frequency Words
Center Games for Up to 6 Players,
Level A • EMC 3380 • © Evan-Moor Corp.

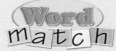

### Game 6 • Caller's Cards

High-Frequency Words
Center Games for Up to 6 Players,
Level A • EMC 3380 • © Evan-Moor Corp.

### Game 6 • Caller's Cards

High-Frequency Words
Center Games for Up to 6 Players,
Level A • EMC 3380 • © Evan-Moor Corp.

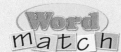

### Game 6 • Caller's Cards

High-Frequency Words
Center Games for Up to 6 Players,
Level A • EMC 3380 • © Evan-Moor Corp.

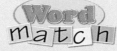

### Game 6 • Caller's Cards

High-Frequency Words
Center Games for Up to 6 Players,
Level A • EMC 3380 • © Evan-Moor Corp.

### Game 6 • Caller's Cards

High-Frequency Words
Center Games for Up to 6 Players,
Level A • EMC 3380 • © Evan-Moor Corp.

Caller's Board

| black | blue | brown |
| down | four | in |
| on | one | out |
| red | three | two |
| up | white | yellow |

## Game 6

High-Frequency Words
Center Games for Up to 6 Players, Level A
EMC 3380 • © Evan-Moor Corp.

Name _____

# What a Big Nose!

Cut. Match. Glue.

Name _____

# Let's Eat!

Draw a line to match.

1.

2.

3.

4.

5.

6.

     High-Frequency Words: Center Games for Up to 6 Players, Level A • EMC 3380 • © Evan-Moor Corp.

# PING PANG POW!

## Play

1. Assign three players to each set.

2. The first player picks a word card from bag 1, reads it aloud, places it in box 1 on the board, and says, "Ping."

3. The next player picks a word card from bag 2 and reads it aloud. If it matches the word in box 1, the player places the card in box 2 and says, "Pang." Then the player goes to step 5.

4. If the words do <u>not</u> match, the player puts the card back into bag 2, and the next player draws a card from bag 2. Play continues until a match is made.

5. The player who makes the match in box 2 draws a card from bag 3. The player reads the word aloud. If the word card is a match, the player places it in box 3 and calls out, "Pow! I win!"

6. If the card does <u>not</u> match, the player puts the card back into bag 3, and play continues until a player draws the winning card.

7. The winning player keeps all three cards, and a new game begins.

## Set A players need:

- Game board
- 21 word cards
- 3 brown paper bags

## Set B players need:

- Game board
- 21 word cards
- 3 brown paper bags

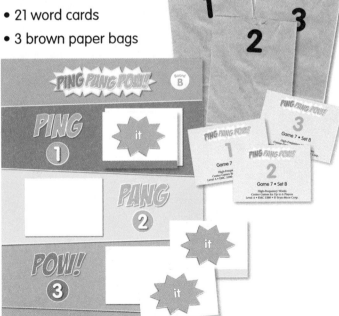

# PING
### 1

# PANG
### 2

# POW!
### 3

## Game 7

High-Frequency Words
Center Games for Up to 6 Players, Level A
EMC 3380 • © Evan-Moor Corp.

# PING PANG POW!

## PING
**1**

## PANG
**2**

## POW!
**3**

## Game 7

High-Frequency Words
Center Games for Up to 6 Players, Level A
EMC 3380 • © Evan-Moor Corp.

| saw | saw | saw |
|-----|-----|-----|
| like | like | like |
| and | and | and |

**PING PANG POW!**

# 3

Game 7 • Set A

High-Frequency Words
Center Games for Up to 6 Players
Level A • EMC 3380 • © Evan-Moor Corp.

**PING PANG POW!**

# 2

Game 7 • Set A

High-Frequency Words
Center Games for Up to 6 Players
Level A • EMC 3380 • © Evan-Moor Corp.

**PING PANG POW!**

# 1

Game 7 • Set A

High-Frequency Words
Center Games for Up to 6 Players
Level A • EMC 3380 • © Evan-Moor Corp.

**PING PANG POW!**

# 3

Game 7 • Set A

High-Frequency Words
Center Games for Up to 6 Players
Level A • EMC 3380 • © Evan-Moor Corp.

**PING PANG POW!**

# 2

Game 7 • Set A

High-Frequency Words
Center Games for Up to 6 Players
Level A • EMC 3380 • © Evan-Moor Corp.

**PING PANG POW!**

# 1

Game 7 • Set A

High-Frequency Words
Center Games for Up to 6 Players
Level A • EMC 3380 • © Evan-Moor Corp.

**PING PANG POW!**

# 3

Game 7 • Set A

High-Frequency Words
Center Games for Up to 6 Players
Level A • EMC 3380 • © Evan-Moor Corp.

**PING PANG POW!**

# 2

Game 7 • Set A

High-Frequency Words
Center Games for Up to 6 Players
Level A • EMC 3380 • © Evan-Moor Corp.

**PING PANG POW!**

# 1

Game 7 • Set A

High-Frequency Words
Center Games for Up to 6 Players
Level A • EMC 3380 • © Evan-Moor Corp.

| was | was | was |
|:---:|:---:|:---:|
| to | to | to |
| they | they | they |

**3**

Game 7 • Set A

High-Frequency Words
Center Games for Up to 6 Players
Level A • EMC 3380 • © Evan-Moor Corp.

**2**

Game 7 • Set A

High-Frequency Words
Center Games for Up to 6 Players
Level A • EMC 3380 • © Evan-Moor Corp.

**1**

Game 7 • Set A

High-Frequency Words
Center Games for Up to 6 Players
Level A • EMC 3380 • © Evan-Moor Corp.

**3**

Game 7 • Set A

High-Frequency Words
Center Games for Up to 6 Players
Level A • EMC 3380 • © Evan-Moor Corp.

**2**

Game 7 • Set A

High-Frequency Words
Center Games for Up to 6 Players
Level A • EMC 3380 • © Evan-Moor Corp.

**1**

Game 7 • Set A

High-Frequency Words
Center Games for Up to 6 Players
Level A • EMC 3380 • © Evan-Moor Corp.

**3**

Game 7 • Set A

High-Frequency Words
Center Games for Up to 6 Players
Level A • EMC 3380 • © Evan-Moor Corp.

**2**

Game 7 • Set A

High-Frequency Words
Center Games for Up to 6 Players
Level A • EMC 3380 • © Evan-Moor Corp.

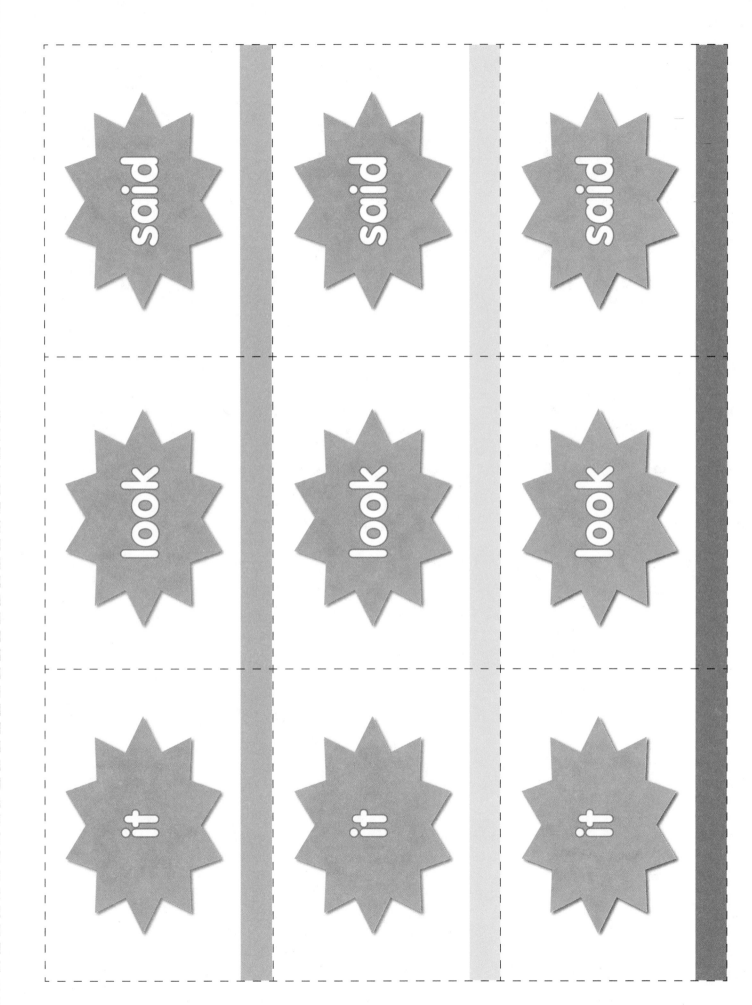

PING PANG POW!

**3**

Game 7 • Set B

High-Frequency Words
Center Games for Up to 6 Players
Level A • EMC 3380 • © Evan-Moor Corp.

---

PING PANG POW!

**2**

Game 7 • Set B

High-Frequency Words
Center Games for Up to 6 Players
Level A • EMC 3380 • © Evan-Moor Corp.

---

PING PANG POW!

**3**

Game 7 • Set B

High-Frequency Words
Center Games for Up to 6 Players
Level A • EMC 3380 • © Evan-Moor Corp.

---

PING PANG POW!

**1**

Game 7 • Set B

High-Frequency Words
Center Games for Up to 6 Players
Level A • EMC 3380 • © Evan-Moor Corp.

---

PING PANG POW!

**2**

Game 7 • Set B

High-Frequency Words
Center Games for Up to 6 Players
Level A • EMC 3380 • © Evan-Moor Corp.

---

PING PANG POW!

**3**

Game 7 • Set B

High-Frequency Words
Center Games for Up to 6 Players
Level A • EMC 3380 • © Evan-Moor Corp.

---

PING PANG POW!

**1**

Game 7 • Set B

High-Frequency Words
Center Games for Up to 6 Players
Level A • EMC 3380 • © Evan-Moor Corp.

---

PING PANG POW!

**2**

Game 7 • Set B

High-Frequency Words
Center Games for Up to 6 Players
Level A • EMC 3380 • © Evan-Moor Corp.

---

PING PANG POW!

**1**

Game 7 • Set B

High-Frequency Words
Center Games for Up to 6 Players
Level A • EMC 3380 • © Evan-Moor Corp.

the

the

the

that

that

that

PING PING POW!

**3**

Game 7 • Set B

High-Frequency Words
Center Games for Up to 6 Players
Level A • EMC 3380 • © Evan-Moor Corp.

Level A • EMC 3380 • © Evan-Moor Corp.

PING PING POW!

**2**

Game 7 • Set B

High-Frequency Words
Center Games for Up to 6 Players
Level A • EMC 3380 • © Evan-Moor Corp.

PING PING POW!

**1**

Game 7 • Set B

High-Frequency Words
Center Games for Up to 6 Players
Level A • EMC 3380 • © Evan-Moor Corp.

PING PING POW!

**3**

Game 7 • Set B

High-Frequency Words
Center Games for Up to 6 Players
Level A • EMC 3380 • © Evan-Moor Corp.

PING PING POW!

**2**

Game 7 • Set B

High-Frequency Words
Center Games for Up to 6 Players
Level A • EMC 3380 • © Evan-Moor Corp.

PING PING POW!

**1**

Game 7 • Set B

High-Frequency Words
Center Games for Up to 6 Players
Level A • EMC 3380 • © Evan-Moor Corp.

Name _____

# Is that You?

Cut. Match. Glue.

you

was

and

like

saw

they

and  like  they  saw  was  you

# That Is for Me!

Draw a line to match.

1.    it

2.    the

3.    is

4.    look

5.    that

6.    said

| | |
|---|---|
| A | for |
| a | funny |
| and | go |
| away | help |
| big | here |
| blue | I |
| can | in |
| come | is |
| down | it |
| find | jump |

| little | said |
| look | see |
| make | the |
| me | three |
| my | to |
| not | two |
| one | up |
| play | we |
| red | where |
| run | yellow |

High-Frequency Words
Center Games for Up to 6 Players, Level A
EMC 3380 • © Evan-Moor Corp.

High-Frequency Words
Center Games for Up to 6 Players, Level A
EMC 3380 • © Evan-Moor Corp.

| | |
|---|---|
| you | came |
| all | did |
| am | do |
| are | eat |
| at | four |
| ate | get |
| be | good |
| black | have |
| brown | he |
| but | into |

High-Frequency Words
Center Games for Up to 6 Players, Level A
EMC 3380 • © Evan-Moor Corp.

High-Frequency Words
Center Games for Up to 6 Players, Level A
EMC 3380 • © Evan-Moor Corp.

| | |
|---|---|
| like | ran |
| must | ride |
| new | saw |
| no | say |
| now | she |
| on | so |
| our | soon |
| out | that |
| please | there |
| pretty | they |

this

too

under

want

was

well

went

what

white

who

will

with

yes

High-Frequency Words
Center Games for Up to 6 Players, Level A
EMC 3380 • © Evan-Moor Corp.

High-Frequency Words
Center Games for Up to 6 Players, Level A
EMC 3380 • © Evan-Moor Corp.

Word Wall Cutouts

Note: Reproduce pages 135–143 to make the word wall.

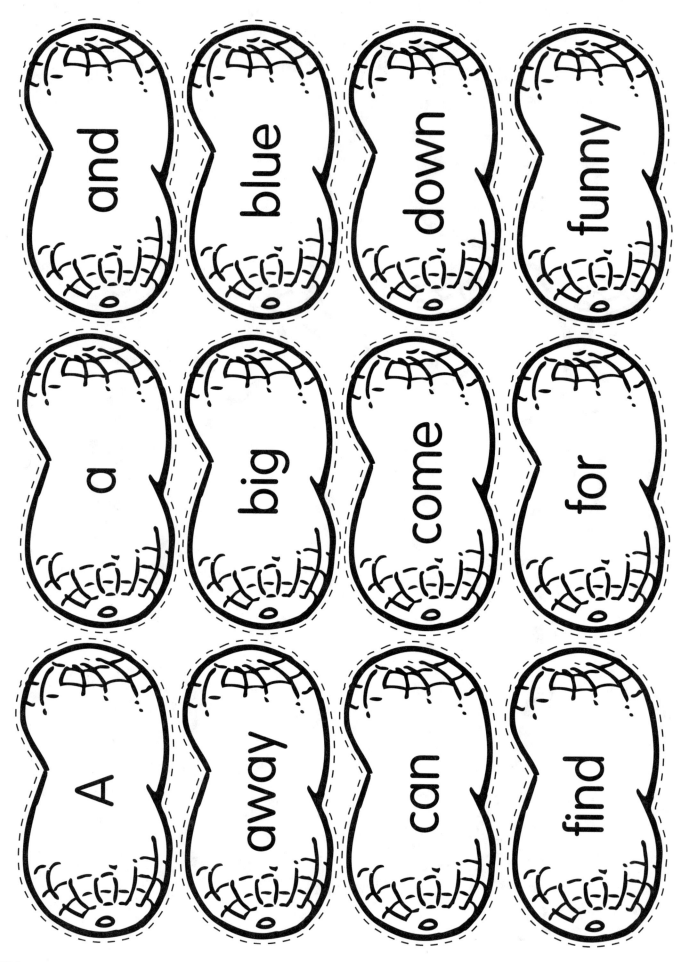

and

blue

down

funny

a

big

come

for

A

away

can

find

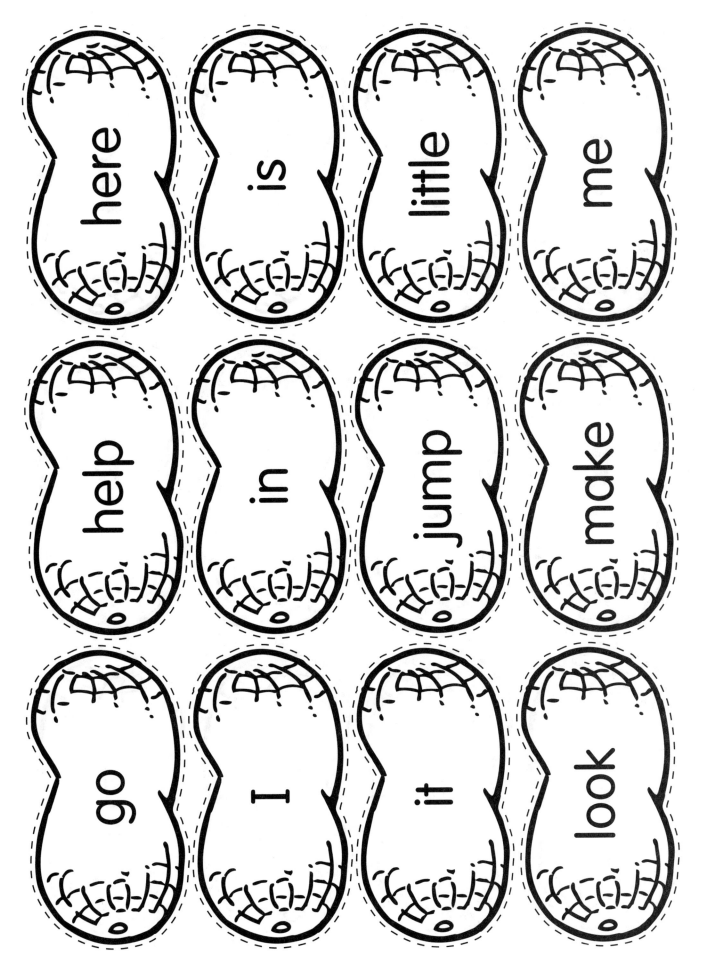

here

is

little

me

help

in

jump

make

go

I

it

look

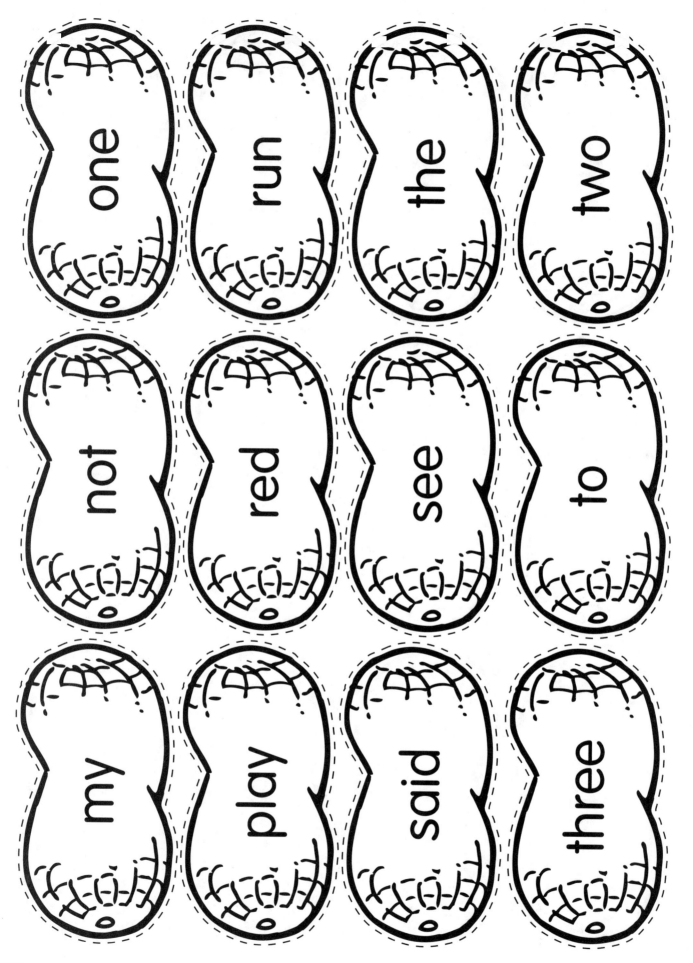

one

run

the

two

not

red

see

to

my

play

said

three

EMC 3380 • © Evan-Moor Corp.

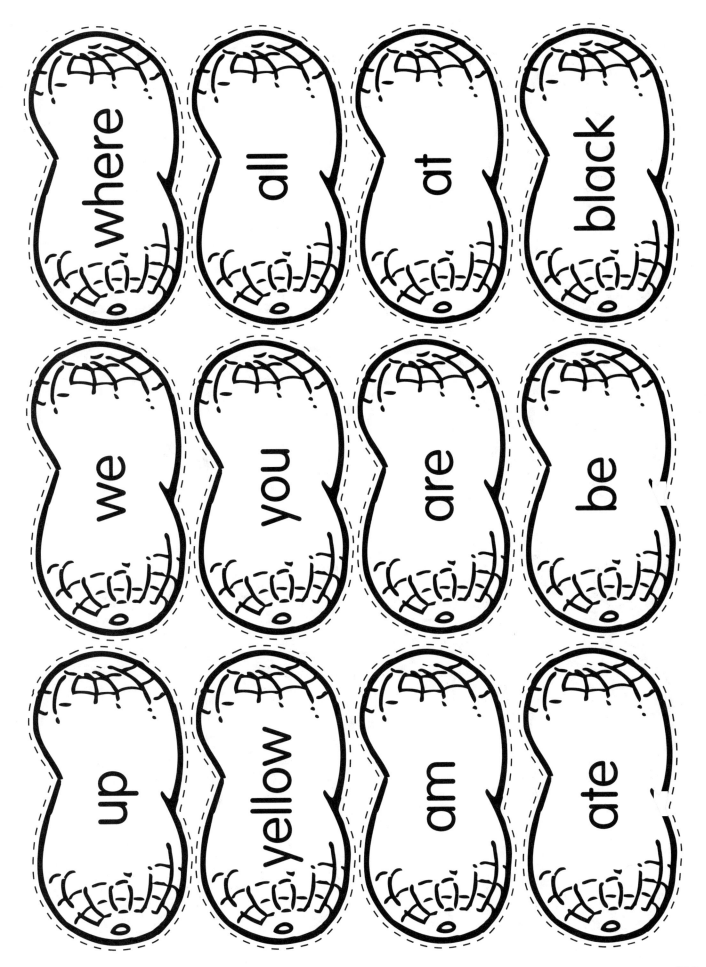

where

all

at

black

we

you

are

be

up

yellow

am

ate

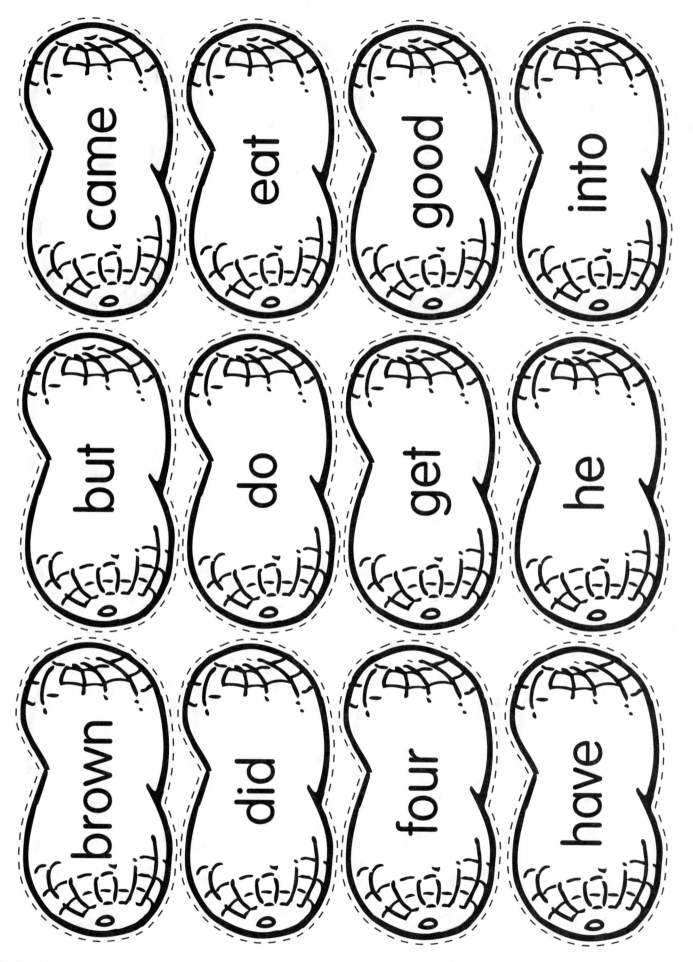

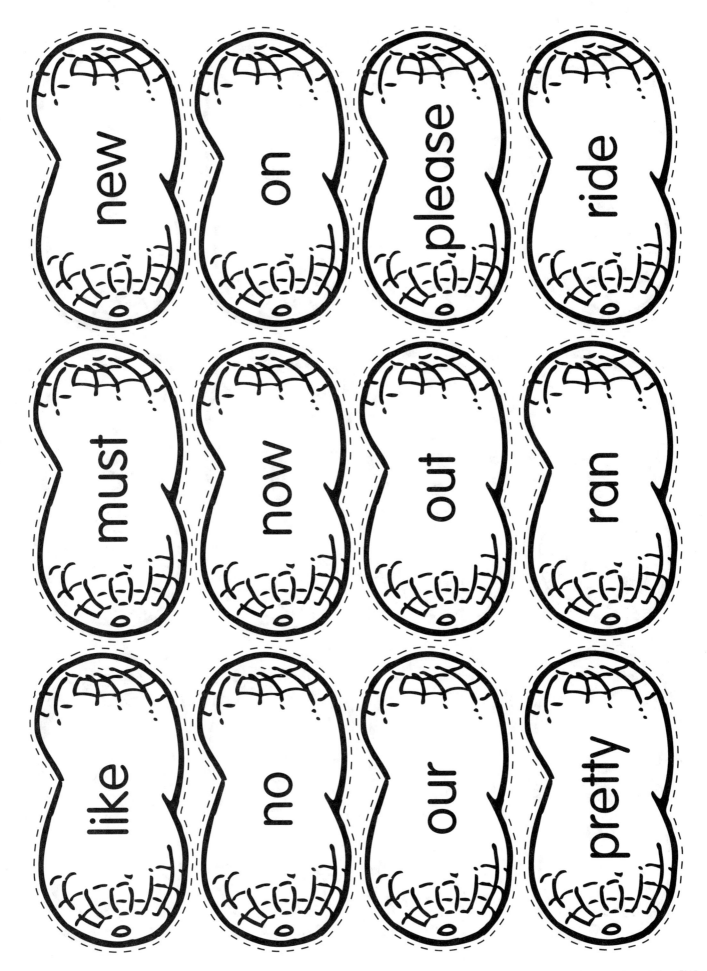

new

on

please

ride

must

now

out

ran

like

no

our

pretty

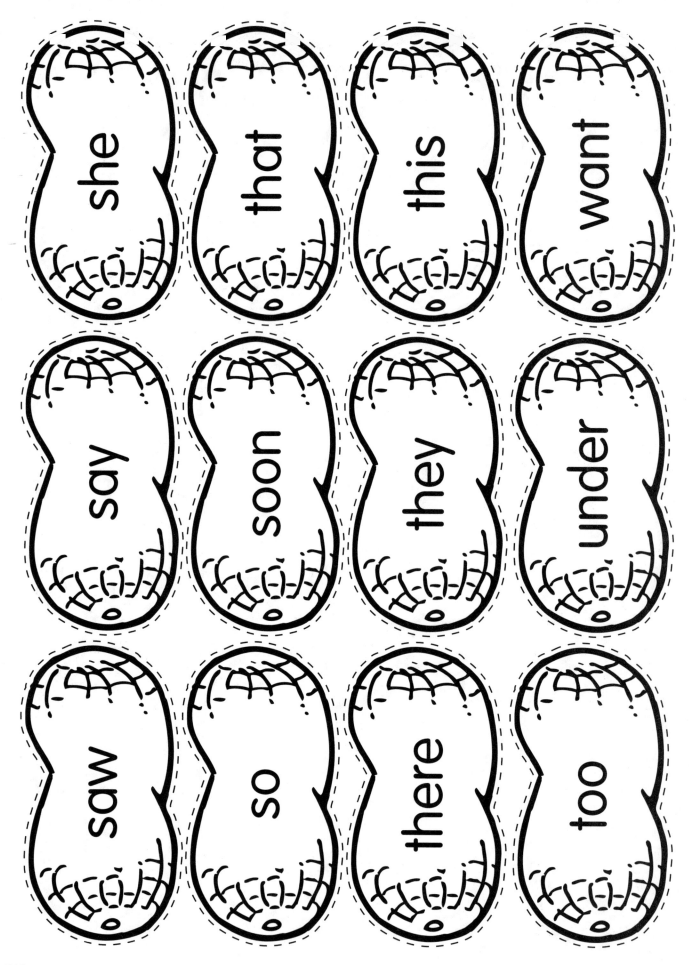

she

that

this

want

say

soon

they

under

saw

so

there

too

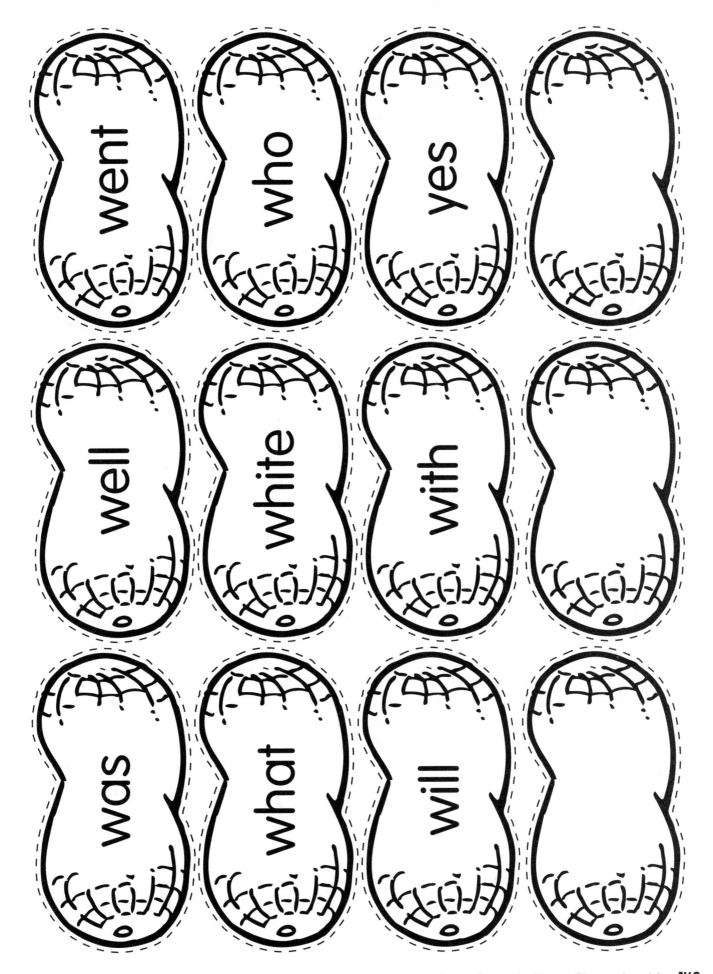

went

who

yes

well

white

with

was

what

will

## Phonics Games:
### *Centers for Up to 6 Players*

This exciting new series supports the skills practiced in our best-selling *Basic Phonics Skills*. The colorful and engaging game formats provide students with the motivation they need to get excited about practicing important phonics skills. Levels A through D sequentially practice phonics skills, beginning with phonemic awareness and ending with structural analysis. 144 full-color pages.
**Correlated to state standards.**

| | | |
|---|---|---|
| **Level A,** Grades PreK–K | EMC 3362 |
| **Level B,** Grades K–1 | EMC 3363 |
| **Level C,** Grades 1–2 | EMC 3364 |
| **Level D,** Grades 2–3 | EMC 3365 |

## Math Games:
### *Centers for Up to 6 Players*

Math practice that's full-color fun! Help your students develop a thorough mastery of grade-level math concepts with 7 hands-on games! Each game comes with an illustrated full-color directions page, game boards and/or playing cards, and 2 reproducible practice pages to reinforce the skills practiced.
**Correlated to state standards.**

| | | |
|---|---|---|
| **Level A,** Grades K–1 | EMC 3029 |
| **Level B,** Grades 1–2 | EMC 3030 |
| **Level C,** Grades 2–3 | EMC 3031 |
| **Level D,** Grades 3–4 | EMC 3032 |